GW00503744

Of Mice and Men

This novel was written by an American called John Steinbeck, who was interested in the plight of ordinary people at a time of real hardship and uncertainty. The story is set in California during the Great Depression in the 1930s, when more than fifteen million workers had lost their jobs.

As you read through each section of the novel, you will be asked to work through a number of tasks and questions. Following this, there will be opportunities for you to review the novel as a whole. As you read, you will develop your skills as:

SPEAKERS AND LISTENERS

by using drama strategies to engage with the characters and their situations
by discussing sections of the novel in various groups, formally and informally
by listening to and commenting on other people's ideas

READERS

by studying a modern classic by a Nobel prize-winning American author
by using evidence to read between the lines
by closely analysing the way spoken language is used

WRITERS

by preparing a dossier (a file of information and evidence) on the central characters
by planning, drafting and completing coursework
by practising examination skills such as note-taking and revision

ENGLISH DEPARTMENT

This study book takes you through the novel, one section at a time. When you have finished, you will be asked to imagine yourself as a member of a Commission of Enquiry, investigating the plight of ranch workers in California in the 1930s. At the enquiry, the personalities, actions and working conditions of each of the characters will be investigated. You will, therefore, need to prepare a 'dossier', a collection of written information and evidence, which you can refer to if you are required to appear at the enquiry.

You should bear this in mind as you work through the book, making sure that your notes are sufficiently well organised for you to retrieve any information that you might need.

In most editions, the book is not divided into specific chapters. As the story moves from one setting to the next, there is merely a gap in the text.

THE POOL – LATE THURSDAY EVENING

Read the first section of the novel which ends with the sentence, '...the sycamore leaves whispered in a little night breeze.'

'A few miles south of Soledad, the Salinas River drops in close to the hill-side bank and runs deep and green.'

A lot of this initial section is written in dialogue. A good way to find out more about the two characters introduced in this section is to prepare a dramatic reading of the scene. This will provide you with initial insights for your dossier. Look, in particular, at the following exchange:

'George,' very softly. No answer. 'George!'

'Whatta you want?'

'I was only foolin', George. I don't want no ketchup. I wouldn't eat no ketchup if it was right here beside me.'

'If it was here, you could have some.'

'But I wouldn't eat none, George. I'd leave it all for you. You could cover your beans with it and I wouldn't touch none of it.'

George still stared morosely at the fire. 'When I think of the swell time I could have without you, I go nuts. I never get no peace.'

Lennie still knelt. He looked off into the darkness across the river. 'George, you want I should go away and leave you alone?'

'Where the hell could you go?'

'Well I could. I could go off in the hills there. Some place I'd find a cave.'

'Yeah? How'd you eat. You ain't got sense enough to find nothing to eat.'

'I'd find things, George. I don't need no nice food with ketchup. I'd lay out in the sun and nobody'd hurt me. An' if I foun' a mouse, I could keep it. Nobody'd take it away from me.'

George looked quickly and searchingly at him. 'I been mean, ain't I?'

GEORGE AND LENNIE

- Clear a space in the middle of the room. You will need two volunteers to be George and Lennie. As a class, help the volunteers to bring the dialogue to life by suggesting physical positioning, facial expressions, tone of voice and movement.

- When you are satisfied with the reading, move into groups of three with one person as director. Choose a different page of dialogue to rehearse together and perhaps perform to the class. This technique, whereby a few volunteers experiment with the dramatic suggestions of the class, is called 'forum theatre'.

LOOKING AT THE SUB-TEXT

- Using the section which your group rehearsed for the dramatic reading, prepare a page of comments about the characters of George and Lennie.

- In order to get a clearer understanding of what is happening in this section as a whole, collect together the sheets produced by each group, photocopy and distribute them. Compare your ideas with those of other groups.

- Having read the sub-text pages from the other groups, what have you learned so far about the characters, the situation they are in and their relationship?

'You remember about us goin' into Murray and Ready's, and they give us work cards and bus tickets?'

'Oh sure, George. I remember that now.' His hands went quickly into his side pockets. He said gently: 'George … I ain't got mine.' He looked down at the ground in despair.

'You never had none, you crazy bastard. I got both of 'em here. Think I'd let you carry your own work card?'

Lennie grinned with relief. 'I … I thought I put it in my side pocket.' His hand went into the pocket again.

George looked sharply at him. 'What'd you take outa that pocket?'

'Ain't a thing in my pocket,' Lennie said cleverly.

'I know there ain't. You got it in your hand. What you got in your hand – hidin' it?'

'I ain't got nothin', George. Honest.'

COMMENTS

-
- George swears a lot, showing his frustration

- Lennie plays a game with George, like a devious child

HELP

The word 'sub-text' literally means 'under the text'. When we read literature, we are constantly picking up clues about what is going on, almost without realising what we are doing. These insights help us to make sense of the text. By becoming aware of the sub-text, we can begin to form our own interpretation of the book.

George plans the timing of their approach to the ranch very carefully so that they can have one night of freedom in the open air. The time he and Lennie spend by the pool is obviously very important to them despite the frustrations of their situation.

TIME OUT

In order to help you begin your dossier file on George and Lennie, consider the questions below. In pairs, discuss your responses to them in preparation for your character studies.

GEORGE

Character

- Why is the time out so important to George?

- What do you learn about George's personality from the way he speaks?

- What evidence can you find to support the view that George is an intelligent man?

Situation

- What seems to have happened to George in the past?

- What are his problems at the moment?

Gary Sinise as George (left) and John Malkovich as Lennie (right), 1992

LENNIE

Character

- Does Lennie enjoy the break under the stars for the same reasons?

- What do you learn about Lennie from the way he behaves and speaks?

- What things are uppermost in Lennie's mind?

Situation

- What seems to have happened to Lennie in the past?

- What are his problems at the moment?

RELATIONSHIP

- Look at the way George speaks to Lennie. How would you describe his attitude to Lennie? Irritation? Affection?

- What does George have to do for Lennie? Why does he do it?

- If George is like a parent to Lennie, is he a good or a bad parent?

HELP

BUILDING CHARACTER STUDIES

A character study will help you organise and record your thoughts and feelings about the characters in the novel. Any character study needs to be supported by evidence from the text. The chart below provides you with a way of organising your ideas and making sure that your opinions can be justified. Having set up a summary chart of this kind for each main character, you will be able to add to it as you read through the rest of the book.

In Column One, there is a set of general points which are useful to note about any character. In Column Two, there is space for you to list relevant sections from the text. This could be a specific quotation or a reference to a moment in the story. Column Three gives you the chance to comment on the evidence by recording your response.

Name of character: Lennie Small		
Findings	**Evidence**	**Comment**
1. Physical characteristics	'a huge man, shapeless of face...'	Steinbeck creates two opposites, who both seem to depend on one another.
2. Background		
3. a) Motivation		
b) Thought processes		
c) Preoccupations		
d) Relationships		
4. a) Possibilities and potential		
b) Problems	"You remember settin' in that gutter in Howard Street?"	George and Lennie's problems seem to arise out of their poverty and rootlessness.
c) Use of Language		

GEORGE AND LENNIE

- Set up two character profiles, one for George and one for Lennie.

- Use the findings of your paired discussions to summarise the main points about George and Lennie.

- Think about why Steinbeck has created these particular characters. In some ways they are complete opposites but they seem to depend on each other and their problems arise in part from their common poverty and rootlessness.

Towards the end of the first section, we learn about George and Lennie's shared dream. Their lives are so harsh that they often take refuge in this dream:

'Guys like us, that work on ranches, are the loneliest guys in the world. They got no family. They don't belong no place. They come to a ranch an' work up a stake and then they go inta town and blow their stake, and the first thing you know they're poundin' their tail on some other ranch. They ain't got nothing to look ahead to.'

Lennie was delighted. 'That's it – that's it. Now tell how it is with us.'

George went on. 'With us it ain't like that. We got a future. We got somebody to talk to that gives a damn about us. We don't have to sit in no bar-room blowin' in our jack jus' because we got no place else to go. If them other guys gets in jail they can rot for all anybody gives a damn. But not us.'

Lennie broke in. *'But not us! Because... because I got you to look after me, and you got me to look after you, and that's why.'* He laughed delightedly. 'Go on now, George.'

'You got it by heart. You can do it yourself.'

'No, you. I forget some a' the things. Tell about how it's gonna be.'

'OK. Some day – we're gonna get the jack together and we're gonna have a little house and a couple of acres an' a cow and some pigs and...'

'An' live off the fatta the lan',' Lennie shouted. *'An' have rabbits.'*

What	**Why**
a couple of acres...	*...because they have never owned their own land.*

The Dream

THE DREAM

- Copy the illustration above on to your own paper. On the left hand side, underneath the word 'What?', note down the features of George and Lennie's dream farm which you learn from their conversation here. Opposite these features, under the word 'Why?', write down the reasons why they are so important to these two characters. An example is provided.

Over the last few pages you have been reading about George and Lennie as if they were real characters. But remember, John Steinbeck created them at a particular time in American history because he wanted to explore the themes of power, ownership and control and their effect upon ordinary people, people who strive for a better life and who have hopes and dreams.

Lennie and George's dream is significant because it tells us something about the culture that has created them. America has always been seen as a land of opportunity, partly because immigrants from Europe saw it as a place of freedom, a place to begin a new life, a place where there were real possibilities for wealth and prosperity for all. This belief in America as a country where ordinary people could create a better life for themselves is often referred to as 'The American Dream'.

'We hold these truths to be self-evident, that all men are created equal, that they are endowed by their Creator with certain unalienable rights, that among these are life, liberty and the pursuit of happiness.'

Declaration of Independence (Adopted in Congress 4th July, 1776)

'Four score and seven years ago our fathers brought forth, upon this continent, a new nation, conceived in liberty, and dedicated to the proposition that 'all men are created equal'. That nation, shall have a new birth of freedom, and that government of the people for the people, shall not perish from the earth.'

Transcript of the Nicolay Draft of the Gettysburg Address

'My fellow Americans, the long dark night for America is about to end.
The time has come for us to leave the valley of despair and climb the mountain so that we may see the glory of the dawn - a new day for America, a new dawn for peace and freedom in the world.'

Richard Nixon: Presidential Nomination Acceptance Speech, 1968

'Give me your tired, your poor, your huddled masses yearning to breathe free,
The wretched refuse of your teeming shore,
Send these, the tempest-tossed, to me:
I lift a lamp beside the golden door.'

*Emma Lazarus
Her poem was written to help raise funds for the construction of the pedestal of the Statue of Liberty in 1903*

THE AMERICAN DREAM

- Study the collection of ideas on page 8. It will help you to begin to understand why Steinbeck included such a powerful dream for his characters.

- Find out all you can about 'The American Dream' in order to make a presentation to the rest of your group. You might do this by creating a collage of images and information taken from film, magazines, literature (poems, novels, plays), political speeches, music and song.

- Before you read on, answer the following questions:

  Are there any hints given in this section which lead you to predict any possible future events in the book?

  How might George and Lennie behave when they finally meet other people?

THE BUNKHOUSE – ABOUT 10 O'CLOCK FRIDAY MORNING

Read the second section of the novel from 'The bunkhouse was a long, rectangular building...' to '...the grizzled head sank to the floor again.'

This first bunkhouse scene introduces us to life on the ranch and the characters who live and work there. It is the first time we see George and Lennie in public. Steinbeck chooses to introduce George and Lennie to six new characters in turn. Each of these new characters is important and has a significant part to play in the novel.

SETTING THE SCENE

In order to consolidate your understanding of the structure of this section, its characters and the theatrical nature of their entrances and exits, you will need to copy and complete the plot wheel below.

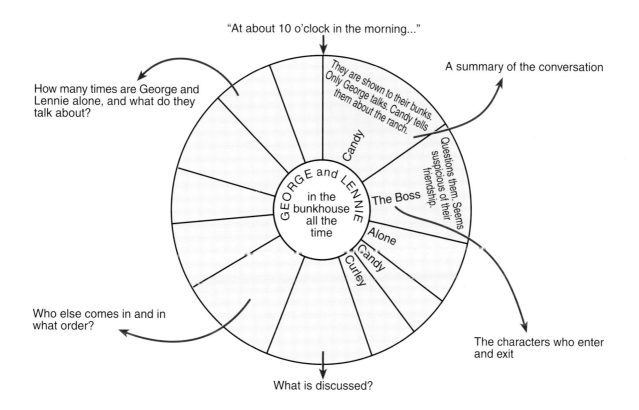

"At about 10 o'clock in the morning..."

They are shown to their bunks. Only George talks. Candy tells them about the ranch.

A summary of the conversation

How many times are George and Lennie alone, and what do they talk about?

Questions them. Seems suspicious of their friendship.

GEORGE and LENNIE in the bunkhouse all the time

Candy

The Boss

Alone

Candy

Curley

Who else comes in and in what order?

The characters who enter and exit

What is discussed?

Your dossier will need information about other people's views concerning George and Lennie. Five of the new characters we meet are men: the old swamper (Candy), the boss, Curley, Slim and Carlson.

FIRST IMPRESSIONS

- In small groups, each dealing with a different character, make notes about the first impression your character receives of Lennie and George.

- As a class, form a circle using each of the small groups. Place two people in the centre to represent George and Lennie. Working round the circle, slowly read the first impressions of each character towards George and Lennie.

- Working on your own, update your dossier.

Charles Bickford as Slim, 1939

In the first bunkhouse scene, George and Lennie also hear about, and then meet, the only female character in the novel, Curley's wife. Look carefully at the way Steinbeck begins to introduce her in this section. How do we first learn of her existence? What do we learn about her? What impression is given?

With Curley's wife, it is important to be clear about what is fact and what is opinion. The chart opposite and the activity associated with it should be used to record your findings as you read through the book.

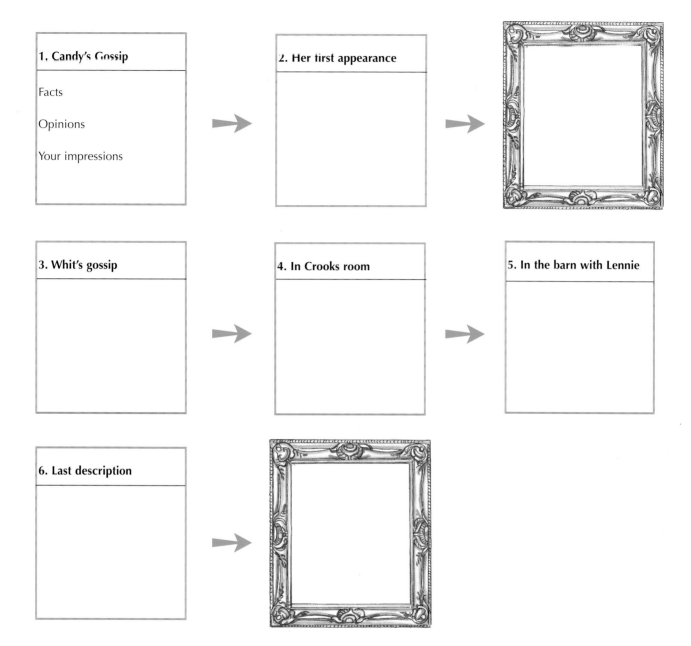

1. Candy's Gossip

Facts

Opinions

Your impressions

2. Her first appearance

3. Whit's gossip

4. In Crooks room

5. In the barn with Lennie

6. Last description

CURLEY'S WIFE

- Draw a chart like the one above. Track down all the references to Curley's wife. Use the boxes to record any facts you can find, any opinions that are expressed and the impression you receive.

- After you have completed the first two boxes, find a picture of a face you feel fits the character so far. You might be able to find an appropriate photograph in a magazine.

- Copy out the remaining boxes which deal with the next significant moments in the text when Curley's wife appears. As you read through the rest of the book, complete these boxes to show how her character unfolds.

- Finally, the last box should be another face, the face that best captures the final impression you have gained.

One of the main reasons why Steinbeck wrote *Of Mice and Men* was to depict the plight of people who are forced to uproot themselves to find work. George and Lennie are obliged to move around to earn the money to stay alive.

Read the following extract together in pairs, taking one voice each.

Lennie cried out suddenly: 'I don't like this place, George. This ain't no good place. I wanna get outa' here.'
'We gotta keep it till we get a stake. We can't help it, Lennie. We'll get out jus' as soon as we can. I don't like it no better than you do.'

What does this extract tell you about the working life of George and Lennie?

WORKING CONDITIONS

- Use the quote above and what you have learnt so far to answer the following questions. Include the answers in your dossier.

1 What do George and Lennie have to go through before they actually start work on the ranch?

2 List the problems of this lifestyle and their current situation.

THE WORKFORCE ON THE RANCH

Since time began, human beings have sought a better life by moving to places which seem to offer some opportunity or the possibility of survival. These migrating people undergo great hardship on their journeys and often encounter hostility in their new land, or place of work. The 1930s, when *Of Mice and Men* was written, was a time of massive unemployment in America and Europe; a time which has been named 'The Great Depression'. There were few jobs to be had and men often had to move around from place to place seeking work.

Ranch work could sometimes be found, but it was seasonal; the job ended when the work was completed. The status of these workers was, therefore, very low. They were paid low wages, had no job security, and had to put up with bad conditions and poor treatment. It was always too easy to find a replacement if they complained or caused trouble. There was no unemployment money in many of the states, and no social security to support people in their struggle to find work and to survive.

The plight of the dispossessed, migrant workers remains the same in some parts of the world. Even today, workers who suffer the same privations as George and Lennie are living and working in Europe. Read the extract below from a study of two European towns.

TURKS IN WEST GERMANY

Sakaltutan is a village of 900 inhabitants in central Turkey. Until recently it was a poor, isolated settlement dependent upon agriculture. With a high birth rate and limited resources the village had become overpopulated. There were too many males to work on the land – women were not expected to work outside the home – and the demand for craftsmen was limited.

Pforzheim is an industrial town near Stuttgart in West Germany. Like other west European towns it had to be rebuilt after 1945 at a time when there were more job vacancies than workers. The extra labour needed was obtained from the poorer parts of southern Europe and the Middle East. Many of these 'guest workers' or *Gastarbeiter* initially went into agriculture as many were originally farmers, but they soon turned to the relatively better paid jobs in factories and the construction industry. These jobs were not taken by the local Germans because they were dirty, unskilled, poorly paid and often demanded long and unsociable hours.

At one stage there were 15 families from Sakaltutan living in Pforzheim. The first arrivals were males in their twenties, all of whom had had some education and were skilled at a craft, making them acceptable in the local car factory or in construction. In an attempt to earn as much money as possible they often took accommodation in poorly equipped company hostels, missed meals and used public transport to reach work.

Now read the lyrics from Bob Dylan's 'Maggie's Farm' on the next page and complete the tasks about migrant workers.

MAGGIE'S FARM

I ain't gonna work on Maggie's farm no more.
No, I ain't gonna work on Maggie's farm no more.
Well, I wake up in the morning,
Fold my hands and pray for rain.
I got a head full of ideas
That are drivin' me insane.
It's a shame the way she makes me scrub the floor.
I ain't gonna work on Maggie's farm no more.

I ain't gonna work for Maggie's brother no more.
No, I ain't gonna work for Maggie's brother no more.
Well, he hands you a nickel,
He hands you a dime,
He asks you with a grin
If you're havin' a good time,
Then he fines you every time you slam the door.
I ain't gonna work for Maggie's brother no more.

I ain't gonna work on Maggie's farm no more.
No, I ain't gonna work on Maggie's farm no more.
Well, I try my best
To be just like I am,
But everybody wants you
To be just like them.
They sing while you slave and I just get bored.
I ain't gonna work on Maggie's farm no more.

Bob Dylan

MIGRANT WORKERS

- What problems do these migrant workers and George and Lennie have in common? Make a list of the disadvantages of this sort of working life. What might be the tensions and frustrations of such a life?

- Find examples of other groups of people who have migrated. What were the circumstances? What were they seeking? What were the consequences?

THE BUNKHOUSE – FRIDAY EVENING

Now read from 'Although there was evening brightness...' to '"Well, get the hell out and wash your face"'. This is a lengthy section which covers a continuous piece of action, culminating in Curley's attack on Lennie. You might choose to read it in class as if it were a play, with someone reading the lines of each of the characters: George, Slim, Lennie, Candy, Carlson, Whit and Curley. You will also need a narrator to read the sections in between the dialogue.

TELLING TALES

This long section falls naturally into a number of separate parts, marked by exits, entrances and conversations.

- In small groups, choose a sample of key quotes that could be used to communicate the essential elements of this part of the story as clearly as possible.

- After you have collected your key quotes, present your version of this scene to the rest of the class. If you are feeling adventurous, you might like to incorporate aspects of drama into your presentation, using tableau (see the Help Box below) and simple movement or gesture. These presentations could be recorded on audio or video tape.

- Each of the men would have a slightly different story to tell about the events of that particular evening. Choose one character to focus on. Discuss between you what you think the main points of his story would be and what might be his attitude towards the incidents. Decide who is to be the storyteller and who is to be the listener. Begin the storytelling with the listener saying, 'What happened on Friday evening in the bunkhouse, then?' Try to let the person relating the story tell it without interruption. You could swap over at the end to give the other person a chance to tell their version of the story or to be another character.

HELP

Tableau – sometimes called a 'freeze frame' or 'still image'. Characters take up position as if the camera caught the act. It can be 'brought to life' if necessary, or the drama can be slowed down to reveal character's thoughts about the scene being depicted.

Use your understanding of this scene to update your dossier by adding to the notes you made about the dream farm, Curley's wife and George and Lennie.

CROOKS' ROOM – SATURDAY EVENING

While all of the other men on the ranch are enjoying themselves in the town, a few characters remain behind. For a variety of reasons, they all gather in Crooks' room. Read from 'Crooks, the negro stable buck...' to '...he fell slowly to rubbing his back.'

The whole of this section takes place in the harness-room where Crooks lives. The description provided by Steinbeck is quite detailed and allows the reader to build up a mental picture of the place.

This episode makes plain a lot that has previously remained unstated and provides a great deal of new information for your dossier. Using the questions below to guide you, update your notes about Crooks, Lennie, Curley's wife and relationships on the ranch.

CROOKS

- Read the first five paragraphs of this section where Steinbeck's narrative is very descriptive of Crooks and study the artist's impression of his room. What do you learn about him? List each of the items Steinbeck describes and make a note about what they reveal about Crooks' character.

- In groups of three, one narrating and the other two in role, read through the section where Crooks and Lennie are talking together. As you read, make a brief list of the extra things you learn about Crooks and Lennie as they gradually begin to trust one another.

- Without realising it, Lennie manages to draw Crooks into a number of personal comments about himself. What does this add to the book?

CURLEY'S WIFE

During this section the reader sees a different side to Curley's wife. She treats all of the men in Crooks' room with contempt.

* Copy out and complete the following chart which takes each of the men in turn and analyses her attitude towards them:

	Lennie	Crooks	Candy
How does she address them?			
What attitude does she adopt towards them?			
Why does she behave like this?			

* Go back to your 'Changing Faces' sheet and record another impression of her.

THE DREAM

* When Candy enters, the conversation shifts to a discussion about the dream. For your dossier, briefly describe what the dream means to each of these characters and why it is so important to them.

SOCIAL CONDITIONS

So far, you have looked at the characters in this section as people. Adopting your role as a social investigator, you might want to go one step further and think about how their behaviour is shaped not by their personalities, but by the society in which they are living.

* Look first of all at the way in which these four characters fit into the society of the ranch. What are their particular problems? Why are they excluded from certain activities? What does this suggest about ranch-life in general?

* What does this scene tell us about the plight of black labourers in American society? Look particularly at the attitude Curley's wife adopts towards Crooks and, just as important, his response.

* Although they dream about a better life, all of the characters feel, in some way, trapped by their circumstances. What is it about the system that contributes towards this?

THE BARN– SUNDAY EVENING

By the end of this section, Curley's wife is dead. Her body is found by Candy, who immediately fetches George. They quickly reach the only possible conclusion, that her death has been caused by Lennie.

There are, however, no witnesses to the events in the barn, nobody to say how it happened. An enquiry into her death would have to reconstruct what happened, relying entirely on informed guesswork and logical deduction.

Before reading the section, imagine what conclusion the investigators might reach about the events that led up to the death of Curley's wife. Start by gathering as much evidence as you can.

 The discovery of the body

'Curley's wife lay on her back, and she was half covered with hay ... the meanness and the plannings and the discontent and the ache for attention were all gone from her face. She was very pretty and simple, and her face was sweet and young. Now her rouged cheeks and her reddened lips made her seem alive and sleeping very lightly. The curls, tiny little sausages, were spread on the hay behind her head, and her lips were parted.'

 It is not obvious how she has died, and the first two people to find her make the mistake of thinking that she is still alive. It is only on closer examination that it becomes clear that she has 'a slightly twisted neck' and Slim is the first to appreciate that 'Her neck's bust'.

 When she is found, she is fully clothed, wearing a bright cotton dress and red 'mules'. These are house shoes with high heels, but no sides or back.

 There is one other slight mystery. The dog that lives in the barn is distressed because one of her puppies is missing.

INTERVIEW WITH GEORGE

George has no doubt that Lennie is responsible because of what he knows about Lennie's behaviour and, particularly, the difficulty that he has in dealing with women. That is why he has given Lennie such strict instructions about not having anything to do with Curley's wife.

- What guess might George make about how it happened and what reasons would he give? Produce a witness statement.

INTERVIEW WITH CANDY

Candy not only finds the body of Curley's wife, but also has strong views about how she behaves with men.

- What guess might Candy make about how it happened and what reasons would he give? Produce a witness statement.

THE INVESTIGATOR'S REPORT

You should now have some notes about the evidence that is available from the scene of the crime, and two statements from people who may not have witnessed the murder, but know both the murderer and the victim well.

- Write a full investigator's report on the crime, reconstructing the crime and explaining how and why it happened. Your report should seek to provide an answer to the following questions:

    Why were Lennie and Curley's wife alone in the barn?

Why has the puppy disappeared?

What might Curley's wife have said to Lennie?

What might Lennie have said to Curley's wife?

What event or action could have sparked off the physical attack on Curley's wife?

Was Curley's wife's death accidental or deliberate?

Whose fault do you think the tragedy is now?

[*continued over...*]

HELP

In your report, you are looking for evidence which will help you to explain the emotional changes which the characters undergo and the way they behave. You already have a detailed knowledge of the background and social position of these two characters and you should apply this knowledge to your analysis and explanation of why the tragedy occurs. Try to keep the following stylistic points in mind as you write:

- Avoid the use of 'I' whenever possible and try to write in the third person. This makes your writing more objective and formal.

- Remember that you are writing for a professional audience so explain the actions of the characters and the reasons for their behaviour as logically and carefully as you can.

- Write in the past tense 'He was... ' not 'He is...'. For example, 'When Curley's wife first began to speak to Lennie, he would almost certainly have been suspicious and cautious because of what George had said to him. She might well have broken down his defences by admitting her own loneliness...'

Sherilyn Fenn as Curley's wife, 1992

It is now time for you to read this section in full. Consider your final entries in the part of your dossier which deals with Curley's wife, 'Changing Faces'. Summarise your final impressions of her and find a picture of a face which you now think represents her character.

THE POOL – SUNSET

Read this final section, perhaps by asking for a volunteer to read it aloud to a group. The section can be divided into four distinct elements:

1   The pool

2   Lennie's arrival and torment

3   George and Lennie

4   The ranch workers

You are going to look at each of these elements in turn.

THE POOL

Re-read the opening paragraphs of this section.

The <u>deep green pool</u> of the Salinas River was still in the later afternoon. Already the sun had left the valley to go climbing up the slopes of the Gabilan mountains, and the hill-tops were rosy in the sun. But by the pool among <u>the mottled sycamores</u>, a pleasant shade had fallen.

A water-snake glided smoothly up the pool, twisting its <u>periscope</u> head from side to side; and it swam the length of the pool and came to the legs of a motionless heron that stood in the shallows. A silent head and beak lanced down and plucked it out by the head, and the beak swallowed the little snake while its tail waved frantically.

<u>A far rush of wind sounded</u> and a gust drove through the tops of the trees like a wave. The sycamore leaves turned up their silver sides, the brown, dry leaves on the ground scudded a few feet. And row on row of tiny wind-waves flowed up the pool's green surface.

<u>As quickly as it had come, the wind died and the clearing was quiet again</u>. The heron stood in the shallows, motionless and waiting. Another little water-snake swam up the pool, turning <u>its periscope head</u> from side to side.

Suddenly Lennie appeared out of the brush, and he came as silently as a creeping bear moves. The heron <u>pounded</u> the air with its wings, jacked itself clear of the water and flew off down-river. The little snake slid in among the reeds at the pool's side.

Lennie came quietly to the pool's edge. <u>He knelt down and drank</u>, barely touching his lips to the water. When a little bird skittered over the dry leaves behind him, his head jerked up and he strained toward the sound with eyes and ears until he saw the bird, and then he dropped his head and drank again.

When he was finished, he sat down on the bank, with his side to the pool, so that he could watch the trail's entrance. He embraced his knees and laid his chin down on his knees.

The light climbed on out of the valley and, as it went, the tops of the mountains seemed to blaze with increasing brightness.

THE POOL

* Look closely at the description of the trees, the wind and the creatures. What connections can you find between this section and the rest of the novel? Look at the repetition. As you were reading, what did you think was going to happen to the second grass snake? What is Steinbeck saying here?

* Now look at the underlined words and phrases. Where have you seen them before? What does Steinbeck want you to remember?

* Think about the structure of the novel as a whole. Why does Steinbeck choose to end the novel by the pool. What effect does this have?

* Why, then, has Steinbeck included this piece of descriptive writing? It does a lot more than just set the scene. What other reasons can you give for including it?

LENNIE'S ARRIVAL AND TORMENT

- What technique does Steinbeck use to show the reader exactly what is going on in Lennie's brain?

- Lennie finds it hard to remember things but here his memories are finding a way of being expressed. Is Lennie in control of his memories?

- Earlier in the book you looked at George as a parent. Lennie has also been described as a 'baby'. In what ways is Lennie like a child? What does this passage add to your understanding of the way Lennie views the world around him?

- Update your notes in your chart on Lennie.

GEORGE AND LENNIE

Steinbeck chooses to show Lennie's state of mind but George's thoughts remain hidden. Before moving on to the next task, re-read the section on 'sub-text' on p.4.

- Imagine that the middle of the class circle is the bank by the pool. Two volunteers have taken up position as George and Lennie. Re-create the final three key moments between George and Lennie as frozen pictures (tableaux) focusing on the thoughts going through George's mind. Follow the steps below:

Step 1
'George came quietly out of the brush...'

Your class need to suggest exactly where, and how, to position George at this point. Various people can then give voice to the possible inner thoughts of George just before he joins Lennie.

Step 2
'George turned his head and listened to the shouts...'

Reposition George and think about how the new sounds might change what is happening inside his head.

Step 3
'George shook himself. He said woodenly...'

Add phrases from the text to your tableau: 'If I was alone I could live so easy... I could get a job an' not have no mess', 'Take off your hat, Lennie, the air feels fine', 'Look acrost the river, Lennie, an' I'll tell you so you can almost see it.' In between each of these extracts being read aloud by members of the group, have George give voice to the real thoughts which lie behind the words.

[continued over...]

As well as what is happening in the subtext, there is another important point which you can draw out in your drama here. This is the way in which George's words are read, or, to put it another way, the **tone** he uses (see the Help Box below). Look closely at the clues Steinbeck gives you about the way George is speaking, for example 'woodenly' and 'His voice was monotonous, had no emphasis.' Read his words as you think Steinbeck intends, then answer the questions below:

- What effect does this tone have on the meaning of the words? What has happened to the dream?

- What makes this scene between Lennie and George so moving? As the words are read aloud, look carefully at the pauses and imagine George's emotions.

- Contrast the tone of George's phrases with Lennie's. Look out for the **adverbs** that Steinbeck uses to tell you how Lennie is speaking.

- 'You can't remember nothing that happens, but you remember ever' word I say.' Is this true? Throughout the novel, Lennie learns and repeats George's phrases, but does he understand them? Do you think Lennie ever understood the dream?

HELP

Tone. The words an author uses can tell you how a passage or sentence should be read: angrily, quietly, humorously, woodenly, etc. They are usually adverbs and give a sense of the mood and atmosphere surrounding the action. Tone is used to give more meaning to the words; here, the way they are spoken is as important as the words themselves. The tone of a passage will help you to understand the subtext.

THE RANCH WORKERS

Use the tableau technique to set the scene as the other men walk into the area near the pool. Suggest ideas for the position of George at this point, and use the text to establish the most appropriate positioning of Lennie. Now choose who is to represent Curley, and who Slim, and decide where they are to stand, looking at the scene before them. Then answer the questions below:

- What would be Curley's thoughts as he burst into the clearing? What might he believe has happened? His thoughts could be voiced by the person representing him, or by several members of the class, as he stands motionless, frozen for a moment in time.

- What would Slim be feeling and thinking? Use the same technique to explore the ways in which Slim's thoughts might be different. What clues does Steinbeck give you?

- Update your notes on the characters of Curley and Slim.

Now that you have completed the novel, check back through your notes to see if there is anything you need to update. Make sure your dossier is complete.

THE INVESTIGATION

At the beginning of this study guide, you were asked to imagine yourself as a member of a Commission of Inquiry, investigating the social and economic conditions that affected working people at the time the novel was written. Such groups were actually set up by the government of the day.

Steinbeck himself campaigned on behalf of workers and their families who were suffering at the hands of banks and employers who were sabotaging progress to improve their conditions. In February, 1938, he wrote:

'Do you know what they're afraid of? They think that, if these people are allowed to live in camps with proper sanitary facilities, they will organise and that is the bugbear of the large landowner and corporation farmer. The states and counties will give them nothing because they are outsiders. The crops of any part of this state could not be harvested without these outsiders.'

THE COMMISSION OF ENQUIRY

Imagine that members of the Commission come to Salinas to investigate the conditions and events at the ranch where George and Lennie worked. They wish to find out more about the 'outsiders' who worked there and what led to the deaths of Lennie and Curley's wife.

- Decide who is to play the various roles in this investigation. You will need a small group to represent the members of the Commission of Inquiry and pairs to represent the views of each of the characters who might be able to shed light on the events:

George, Slim, Candy, Crooks, Whit, The Boss, Curley

Other possibilities: the Sheriff, someone from Weed, the bus driver

- Set up your classroom in order to create the more formal atmosphere of an inquiry (see below).

- Open the inquiry by calling for the first character submissions. While members of the Commission are in role taking evidence from the characters, the observers will need to take notes so that the evidence is captured for future use in coursework or revision.

- Once the 'character' has testified, the commission should feel free to probe further and ask them supplementary questions. Look at the Help Box on the next page for guidance.

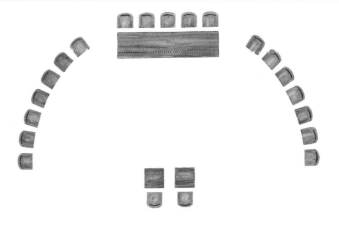

HELP

MEMBERS OF THE COMMISSION

If you are a member of the Commission remember to use your dossier in which you have researched several characters, learnt about existing social and economic conditions and recorded how these have affected the hopes and dreams of ordinary men and women. Use this background information and the following questions to begin your preparations.

1. *Explain who you are, what you do and where you live.*
2. *What do you know about the ranch and what went on there?*
3. *What can you tell the Commission about George and Lennie and the events leading up to Lennie's death?*
4. *What can you tell us about the death of Curley's wife?*
5. *Explain, if you can, how any of this happened.*

WITNESSES TO THE COMMISSION

If you are representing one of the characters, you will be working in a pair to prepare your submission to the inquiry. You will also need to be prepared to answer any supplementary questions they might ask you.

1. *Think about your character as revealed in the novel.*
2. *Consider what you could say about your background, where you work and what you feel about it.*
3. *Is there anything that you are angry or anxious about that you would like the Commission to know?*
4. *Think about what you know about George and Lennie and what you feel about them. How much would you be able to reveal to the Commission?*
5. *What are your thoughts and feelings on the death of Curley's wife?*

The drama work in which you have just been involved provides material for course work of various kinds. It is also, of course, an important example of speaking and listening, and could be used as a major piece of oral work in your course.

   In addition, you may like to write about and record the information you have gathered as a result of the Commission of Inquiry. On the opposite page are three suggestions for written work.

- Working on your own, produce a piece of self-assessment based on the speaking and listening activities undertaken here. You will need to include details of the task, your contributions and achievements and the aspects you might improve next time.

- Write a report based on the findings of the Commission of Inquiry. Below is a suggested layout of the report to help you organise your material.

COMMISSION OF INQUIRY : A REPORT   California 1938

Aim | To investigate conditions affecting workers in the State; to study the lives of particular migrant workers and their particular social and economic conditions.

THE REPORT

A Interviews

Our first discussion was held with a migrant worker named George Milton whose associate, Lennie Small, has been found dead...

B Research

- Current unemployment figures are running at...
-
-
-

C Conclusions

- The death of Curley's wife was a direct result of...
-
-
-
- It is the opinion of the Commission that such tragedies could be avoided if...

- Produce an account written by one of the characters. You should include their version of the interview with the Commission and their inner feelings and thoughts about the two deaths on the ranch. This is called 'writing in role'.

COURSE WORK AND REVISION TASKS

ESSAY WRITING

Select one or more of the following four essays to write as a piece of course work.

- 'Choose three characters from *Of Mice and Men*. What do you learn of their personalities, and what seems to be their role in the novel?'

- 'What do you believe prompted Steinbeck to write his novel *Of Mice and Men*? What themes did he wish to explore by creating the characters, and by including two tragic deaths?'

- '"He would of went south," he said, "We came from north so he would of went south."' With this statement George deliberately misleads Curley; he has also stolen and concealed Carlson's gun. By doing these things he is able to give Lennie a peaceful death. What do these actions say about George's character?

- Read the poem 'To a mouse' by Robert Burns (you will find this on the inside back cover of this book). In this poem Burns is suggesting that even the best laid plans can go wrong. Why do you think Steinbeck has made reference to this poem in the title of this novel?

HELP

As you prepare your course work pieces, you will need to consider the following points about writing an essay.

- Essays are used to discuss ideas and should include evidence that supports these ideas. You will therefore need to use relevant quotations and brief references to points in the story to back up your comments.

- Remember you are responding to a particular question or title. You must answer it; you must follow the instructions closely. So, use the actual words of the title regularly to help you keep to the point in each paragraph.

- Use a formal style rather than a 'chatty' or personal one, and remember to show that you are aware that a writer has created the text. Avoid using the first person (I), for example:

'I think that Curley's wife is an attention-seeker' could become 'Steinbeck portrays Curley's wife as a character who wants to be noticed, who needs company and

attention. The reader gradually discovers this as the novel progresses.'

- Your paragraphs need to be carefully constructed so that each deals with a slightly different point in a logical order. The first sentence of each one needs to introduce the main theme of the paragraph and needs to link in some way with the one before it, for example:

A paragraph might deal with the way George and Lennie talk about the dream farm in the first scene of the novel. The next paragraph could then begin: 'However, in the bunkhouse scene a new dimension is added to their dream; Candy becomes involved...'

- Your essay will also need to begin with an appropriate introduction and end with a proper and effective conclusion. Make the introduction fairly general, defining the terms used in the title perhaps, and make your conclusion sum up your ideas and end on a positive and final note.

REVISION

You may well need to revise the novel in preparation for an examination question on it. There are many useful ways of doing this. Remember, the most effective revision

- involves active reading, i.e. making notes as you read

- is focused, searches for new discoveries about specific characters or themes, and writes them down

- finds new ways of summarising the novel: maps, charts, diagrams, lists, cartoons...

- practises sample examination answers, in note form or in full.

Try some of the following approaches which will help you remember what you need to know in the examination room.

THE CHARACTERS

A useful way of looking at the characters and their role in the novel, is to consider their status, their position in the society of the ranch, their power, or lack of it.

Imagine the line below represents degrees of power on the ranch. Those with least status, power or control over their lives would be placed at the bottom, while those with more power would be higher.

THE STATUS LINE

- Working in a small group, copy the line on to a piece of paper and debate where you feel each of the main characters should be placed and why. Write the characters' names on the left of the line and the reasons on the right.

- Show the class your group's conclusions by using the space in your classroom. An imaginary line on the floor represents the status line on your sheet.

- Now ask for volunteers to represent the characters and place them in the correct position in order to show what your group decided. Explain your decisions to the rest of the class.

- Each group is likely to have chosen a different order. Which characters did the other groups feel differently about?

THE STRUCTURE

One of the most difficult things to get a grasp of when you are revising is the structure of the novel as a whole. *Of Mice and Men* presents particular difficulties as it is just one continuous piece of prose. There are no chapter numbers or headings to break it up and signal the move from one section of the story to another.

A good way of analysing the structure of the book is to think about where events happen. *Of Mice and Men* has a strong sense of place; of a particular pool, bunkhouse, harness room and barn. Putting these on to an annotated map is a useful way of revising, as it helps you to visualise the events and to fix the geography of the novel.

MEMORABLE MAPS

- Look at the descriptive paragraphs that introduce each scene. These will help you to draw a simple map of the places included in the novel. Include insets in which quotations, and possibly drawings, are placed to add relevant detail. Look back at the plan of the harness-room on p16 to help you.

- Annotate your map by listing the main things that happened at each place; think carefully about conversations as well as events.

EXAM QUESTIONS AND ANSWERS

As a final part of your revision, you need to practise answers to exam questions both in note form and in full. Here is a sample question and an example of an answer in note form to help you in your own revision.

'What is the importance of the character of Curley's wife in *Of Mice and Men*? Why do you think she is included?'

① Introduction

Ways in which characters in general become important in a novel, writers' use of them, steinbeck's choice of her.

② Curley's wife

How she is revealed in conversations and gossip, judgements, prejudice of other characters.

③ Her relationships with other characters

Distant, cruel, doesn't fit, outsider. Relationship with Curley, ranch workers, Slim, Crooks.

④ As she is revealed in barn with Lennie

Vulnerable, dreams, hopes.

⑤ Therefore: Links with themes

Loneliness, harshness of ranch society. Why she is included — summary.

Now try producing an outline plan for the following two essay questions.

- 'Choose two characters in *Of Mice and Men* who you feel have particular problems in their lives. Describe and compare them, saying which you feel the most sympathy for.'

- 'All the characters in *Of Mice and Men* are essentially lonely.' Consider three of the characters and Steinbeck's own views in the light of this statement.